Orlando Austin New York San Diego Toronto London

Visit *The Learning Site!*
www.harcourtschool.com

Living and Nonliving

You are a living thing. You need food, water, and air. All **living** things need food, water, and air. Living things grow and change.

All animals are living things. Plants are living things, too.

Fast Fact

Wild elephants need a lot of food. One elephant can eat up to four hundred pounds of food a day!

This animal is a living thing. The plants are living things, too.

Your pencil and this book are nonliving things. A baseball, a rock, and a swing are nonliving things.

Nonliving things do not need food, water, or air. If something does not grow, it is nonliving. You can classify all things as living or nonliving.

COMPARE AND CONTRAST **How is a deer different from a book?**

Mammals

Not all living things are alike. You can group living things in many ways. A living thing can be a plant or an animal. A living thing can be large or small.

There are many different kinds of animals. They have different kinds of bodies and live in very different ways.

Cows and grass are living things. A cow is an animal. Grass is a plant.

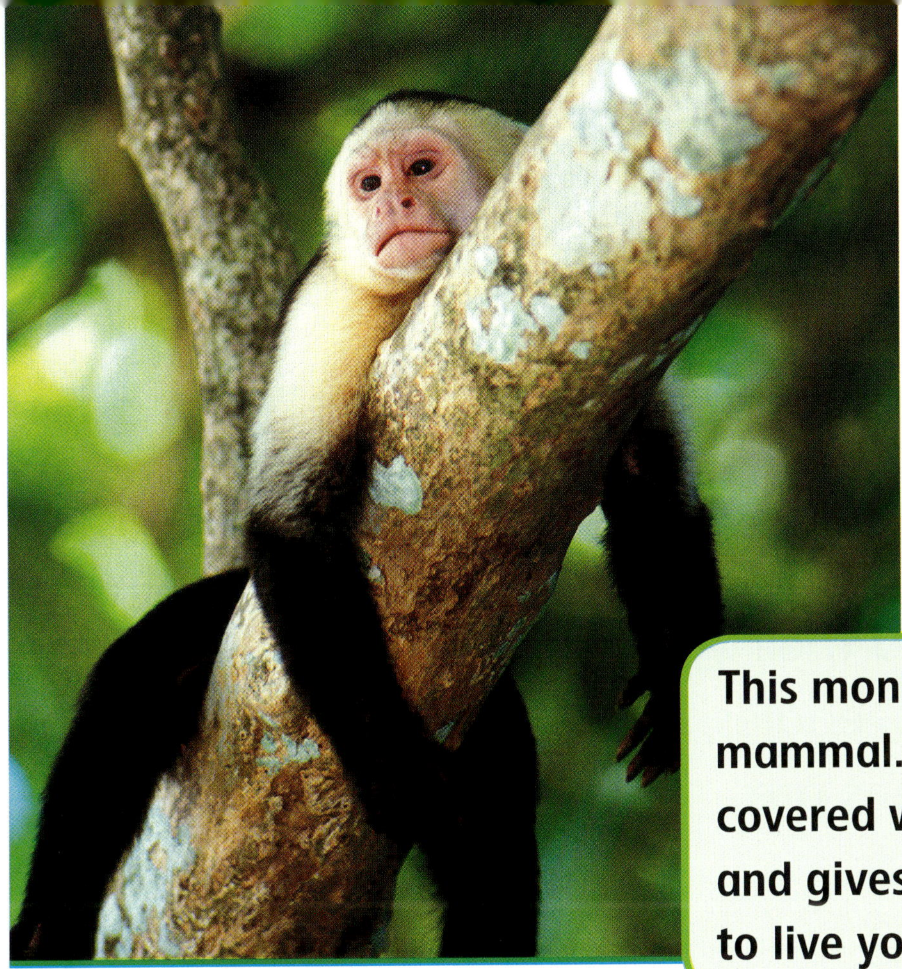

This monkey is a mammal. It is covered with hair and gives birth to live young.

A **mammal** is an animal that has hair or fur. Mammals give birth to live young. The young drink milk from their mothers. Cats, elephants, and bears are mammals.

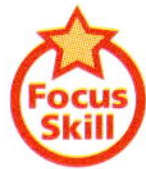

Focus Skill **MAIN IDEA AND DETAILS** How can you tell that a polar bear is a mammal?

Birds and Reptiles

A **bird** is the only kind of animal with feathers. Birds have their young by laying eggs. Most birds use their wings to fly. Birds must go find food to feed their young. Ducks, eagles, and chickens are all birds.

Fast Fact

An ostrich is a bird that does not fly. An ostrich egg is the largest bird egg. It weighs three pounds.

Many birds make a safe place for their young in nests.

A crocodile is a member of the animal group called reptiles. Snakes and lizards are reptiles, too. **Reptiles** have dry, scaly skin. Turtles are reptiles that have shells over their skin.

COMPARE AND CONTRAST **What is one difference between a bird and a reptile?**

Alligators are reptiles. Some can hold their breath underwater for a whole day!

Amphibians and Fish

A frog is a kind of animal, too. It belongs to the group called amphibians. Most **amphibians** have smooth, wet skin. They lay eggs in the water. They move to land when they grow up.

Fast Fact

The longest frog jump was over 33 feet!

A salamander is a kind of amphibian.

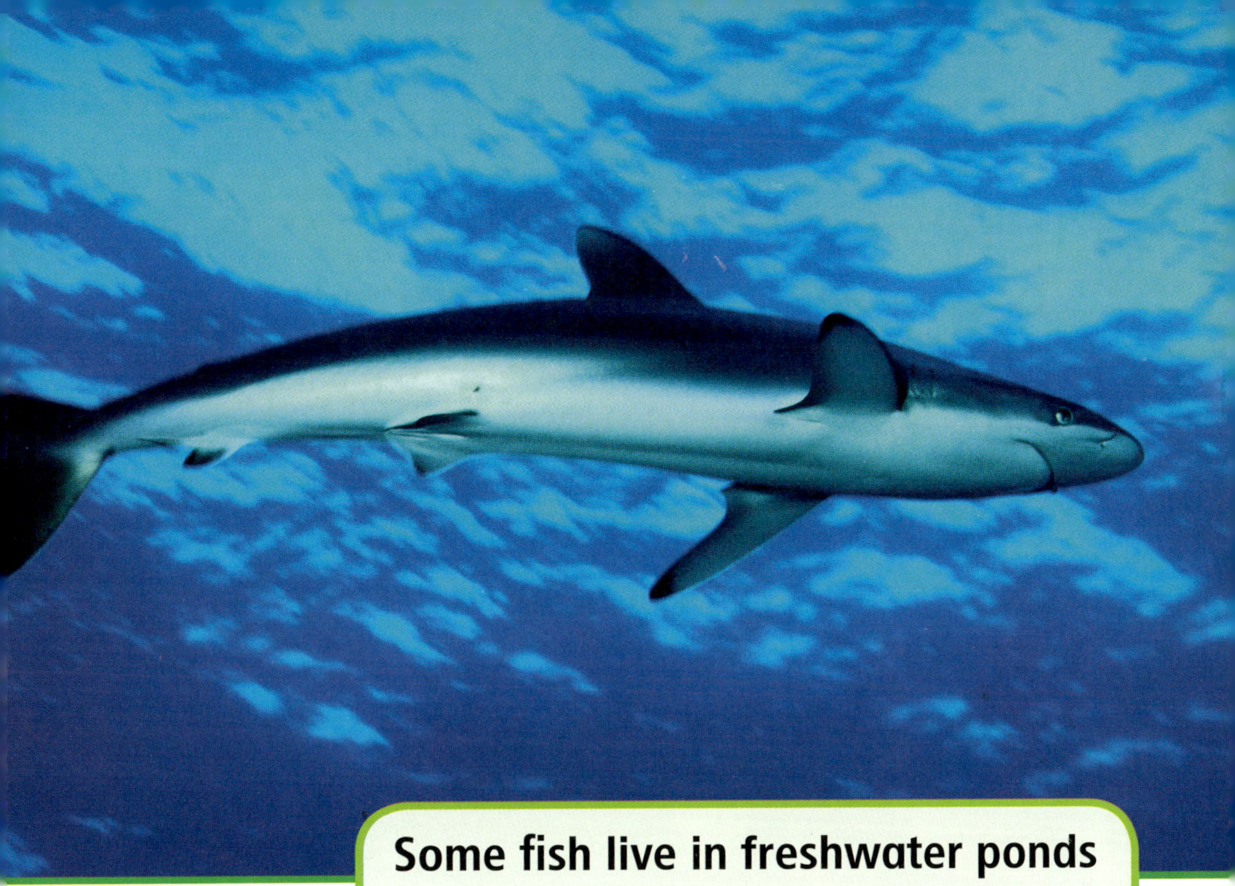

Some fish live in freshwater ponds and rivers. This shark lives only in saltwater. It lives in the ocean.

Fish live in the water. Most **fish** are covered with scales. Fish breathe with gills. Their gills take the air from the water. Sharks, trout, and stingrays are all fish.

MAIN IDEA AND DETAILS **How do fish get air?**

Insects

An **insect** is an animal with six legs and three body parts. Insects have a hard shell to protect their soft insides. They do not have bones. Some insects have wings. Butterflies, ants, and beetles are all insects.

Bees are insects. They often build homes called hives.

Ladybugs are insects. Their hard shells protect their soft insides. Ladybugs can be male or female.

Summary

Animals are living things. Animals can be classified into different groups. The animal groups are mammals, birds, reptiles, amphibians, fish, and insects. Each animal, in every group, needs food, water, and air.

Glossary

amphibian A kind of animal that has smooth, wet skin (8, 11)

bird The only kind of animal that has feathers (6, 7, 11)

fish A kind of animal that is covered in scales, uses gills to breathe, and lives in water (8, 9, 11)

insect A kind of animal that has three body parts and six legs (10, 11)

living Needing food, water, and air to grow and change (2, 3, 4, 11)

mammal A kind of animal that has hair or fur and feeds its young milk (4, 5, 11)

nonliving Not needing food, water, and air and not growing (2, 3)

reptile A kind of animal that has scaly, dry skin (6, 7, 11)